IMAGES
of America

CLEVELAND SLOVAKS

On the cover: Time spent on Kelleys Island with Fr. Vaclav Chaloupka, pastor of the Nativity of the Blessed Virgin Mary Parish, was not without its share of work. Besides fun in the sun and water, children and young adults helped with the various chores, including harvesting some hay. Their Slovak parents, used to an agrarian lifestyle, would have approved. (Courtesy of the Slovak Institute and Library.)

IMAGES
of America

CLEVELAND SLOVAKS

John T. Sabol and Lisa A. Alzo

ARCADIA
PUBLISHING

Published by Arcadia Publishing
Charleston, South Carolina

Library of Congress Control Number: 2008920507

For all general information contact Arcadia Publishing at:
Telephone 843-853-2070
Fax 843-853-0044
E-mail sales@arcadiapublishing.com
For customer service and orders:
Toll-Free 1-888-313-2665

Visit us on the Internet at www.arcadiapublishing.com

*To our Slovak families and Slovak families everywhere, whose dedication
and dreams encouraged many to reach for the stars.*

CONTENTS

ACKNOWLEDGMENTS

We are grateful to the following individuals and organizations for their help in obtaining the photographs that appear in this book: Anniversary Publications Company; Archives of the Diocese of Cleveland and its director, Christine Krosel; the diligent staff at Cleveland Public Library, Photograph Collection; the great resources—human and otherwise—at the Cleveland Press Archives at Cleveland State University; Cyrus and Helen Duval; Edward Ferenc; Andrew Ferko; the late Mary Ann Hisnay; Robert Hlasko; John Hopko; Ellen Howard; Joan Kovalcik; the Lakewood Historical Society; Jim Noga; Louise O'Boyle; Joseph Olsavsky; Our Lady of Mercy Church and Fr. Joseph Hilinski; John T. Sabol; Ronald Seman; St. Andrew Abbey; St. Wendelin Church; Sisters of Charity of Cincinnati; Andrew Hudak, director, and Joseph Hornack, assistant director, of the Slovak Institute and Library, arguably the greatest Slovak cultural and historical resource in the United States; Eileen Sotak; Joan Thesling; the American Slovak Zemplin Social Club; Raymond Tindira; James Virost; Jan Zamiska; and any others we may have inadvertently overlooked.

Since work started on this book, two Cleveland parishes that played key roles in developing Cleveland's Slovak community—Our Lady of Mercy and St. Wendelin—have been designated for closing by the Cleveland Catholic Diocese. SS. Cyril and Methodius Parish and a nearby parish have also been directed to merge at the SS. Cyril and Methodius site. It is not known how much of SS. Cyril and Methodius's Slovak identity will be retained. This process continues at this time.

Another parish, St. Andrew, has also closed and was demolished in 2009.

There are some who know firsthand the time it takes to produce a book such as this—particularly John's wife Jeanne. And there is a Slovak father and relatives in Slovakia who never let John forget his heritage and encouraged him to learn the Slovak language (at least a little).

Lisa would like to thank her Slovak grandparents for their courage and determination to make the journey to America and for passing down all the beautiful Slovak traditions she holds dear.

This work would not have been possible without their persistent—yet unknowing—assistance.

INTRODUCTION

The only record of Cleveland's first Slovak immigrant is an account from Cleveland's second Slovak immigrant, Jacob Gruss, who died in 1939. When Gruss arrived in Cleveland in 1880 with his wife and family, he found one fellow countryman in the city—Jan Roskos. At the time Roskos and Gruss were blazing a trail to Cleveland, most Slovak immigrants were choosing to work in the coal-mining towns of Pennsylvania or West Virginia. Following the advice of an employment agent when he arrived in the United States, Gruss chose to work aboveground and settled on Cleveland, which at the time was the fifth-largest city in the United States with many factory jobs available.

It is not known whether Roskos ever remained in Cleveland, but Gruss did stay to become the first tile in an incredible mosaic of Slovaks, primarily from the eastern part of what was then known as Northern Hungary, part of the Austro-Hungarian Empire. Slovak immigration began in the 1880s, reached its peak at the beginning of the 20th century, and eventually tapered off with the beginning of World War I and the immigration restrictions that followed. Unlike Gruss, who brought his family, the usual pattern would be for men to leave Europe with the hope of making enough money so their family could live comfortably in Europe. Some actually did return to Europe. But the majority found the American dream and sent money to Europe so their wives and children or other members of their families could enjoy life here.

In Europe and when they arrived in America, these early immigrants would have been classified as Hungarians. In their hearts and with their tongues, however, they knew their roots. Yet even upon arrival in America as they sought jobs, these new immigrants faced many employers who never even heard of the term Slovak and had no idea where these new immigrants were from. They lived in boardinghouses run by Slovaks who had made enough money to own property, or perhaps they lived with relatives. But their goal was the same—to own property and to raise their families as English-speaking Americans. At the same time, they never forgot their roots and their language, and they brought with them traditions and music that are still remembered in Cleveland to this day.

Those who followed Jacob Gruss settled in Cleveland near the mills or factories where they would work. They established churches as the anchors for their communities, and many found themselves living near some of the same people who were their neighbors in Europe. Whole families—including parents, brothers, sisters, and cousins—settled within walking distance of each other. Because of the reverence Slovaks have for their religion, the parish hall became the community center.

In Cleveland and neighboring Lakewood, they founded eight Roman Catholic parishes as well as five Lutheran, one Calvinist, and one Baptist church. Many of these are profiled in this book. Besides these, however, Cleveland is home to the headquarters of two major Slovak Catholic fraternal organizations: the First Catholic Slovak Union of the USA and Canada and the First Catholic Slovak Ladies Association. The Slovak League of America was also founded in Cleveland, in 1907, at Gray's Armory.

As World War I and the eventual breakup of the Austro-Hungarian Empire began, Cleveland Slovaks played an integral part in helping to win the war and to establish—for the first time in history—a homeland for the Slovaks. More than 360 Slovaks and Czechs from Cleveland were members of the Czechoslovak legionnaires, who fought in Europe on the western and even the eastern fronts three years before the United States entered the war. At the same time, at the urging of Cleveland pastor Fr. Oldrich Zlamal, Cleveland Slovaks and Czechs began a campaign in 1915 to establish a unified homeland. On October 22, 1915, Slovak and Czech representatives signed the Cleveland Agreement at Cleveland's Bohemian National Hall, which called for a unified federal state of Czechs and Slovaks. This was a prelude to the Pittsburgh Agreement, signed on June 15, 1918, which affirmed more strongly the need to establish what eventually would become the country of Czechoslovakia.

Following World War I, Cleveland's Slovaks continued to establish themselves and their families in America. Their true blossoming into the economic life of the community came after World War II, as the sons and daughters of the immigrant Slovaks sought more for themselves and their families, creating another migration—this time to Cleveland's suburbs. As a result, Slovak churches that were once filled every Sunday became almost-empty monuments, commemorating the hard work and skills of the immigrants who built them. Today Cleveland's remaining Slovak Roman Catholic parishes face a doubtful future because of a reconfiguration of parishes in the Cleveland Catholic Diocese.

Yet the Slovaks, now spread over northeast Ohio, are still a viable force. Slovaks rank number six in population of ethnic groups tracked in the 2000 U.S. census, with 93,495 claiming Slovak ancestry and a median household income of $52,349. According to the census, of people claiming Slovak descent, 84 percent own their own home.

With the demise of ethnic newspapers in every community, Cleveland is no different. However, Cleveland radio stations still have two Slovak-language programs each week. And each year since 1971, a Slovak festival held in Parma, one of Cleveland's highly ethnic suburbs, draws thousands of Slovaks or people who claim to be Slovak at least for the day.

Other monuments to the Slovaks exist in Cleveland, including the Slovak Cultural Garden and a memorial statue to the Slovak hero Gen. Milan Rastislav Stefanik, located at the base of the cultural center of the city, University Circle. At Crown Hill Cemetery is a marker recognizing some serving as World War I legionnaires.

The message from the Slovak community is clear: they are here to stay. Jan Roskos and Jacob Gruss would be proud.

One

FROM THESE ROOTS

Emigration of many Slovak families occurred with single men or husbands coming to America first. After they established themselves, they could afford to bring other family members here. The Andrew Ferenc family was no different, although their journey took a little longer. Andrew Ferenc Sr. (third from the left) arrived in the United States in 1911, leaving his pregnant wife Mary (left) in Kassabela, Austria-Hungary (Košická Belá, Slovakia). World War I intervened, and he would have to wait until 1920 before he could send for his wife and nine-year-old son (second from the left) to come to Cleveland. To remind himself of his family in Europe, Andrew Ferenc had this composite constructed from five other photographs. (Courtesy of John T. Sabol.)

Emilia Hlasko (left) is shown with her mother and grandmother and brothers Julius and John Hlasko in Rovné Czechoslovakia in the 1920s. Emilia would immigrate to the United States and Cleveland in 1938. (Courtesy of Robert Hlasko.)

Joseph Olsavsky from Oskov, Czechoslovakia, and his wife Anna (Kutney) Olsavsky from Bartošovce, Czechoslovakia, are shown with their daughter Mary around 1923. Joseph Olsavsky worked for the American Steel and Wire Company, and they were parishioners at St. Wendelin Church. A copy of this photograph would probably have been sent back to Bartošovce to let their families know that they had made a good life for themselves in America. (Courtesy of Joseph Olsavsky.)

No. 11273   Cleveland, O. *April 28* 19*10*

Received from *John and Anda* at *2057 Robin*

Ten + 45/100   Dollars

For (Foreign Currency) *50. Kronen*

To be remitted to *Monyak Janos*

Address *Felso Zubricza*

Arva Megye Hungary

$ *10.45*   per *Snahnican*

ANTON SNAHNICAN
Steamship Agent and Foreign Exchange
12228 Plover, corner Lark St. — LAKEWOOD, OHIO

Once Slovak families established themselves in the United States, they often shared their newfound "wealth" with family members in their home village. This receipt for $10.45 was processed by a travel agent at the corner of Plover and Lark Avenues in Lakewood's Birdtown and would have brought the family in Felso-Zubricza, Hungary, 50 crowns. Felso-Zubricza is close to the Slovak border with Poland. (Courtesy of Louise O'Boyle.)

John Antonik (wearing his sheepskin coat) came to the United States with his wife and children from Nižny Hrušov in Zemplin County, Hungary, settling first in northeast Pennsylvania before moving to Cleveland. The family settled in the Buckeye Road area, although John and his wife later lived with a daughter either on her farm or at her home on Parkview Avenue. (Courtesy of Eileen Sotak.)

The Joseph Hornak family, living on Lamontier Avenue in 1922, is an example of Cleveland's Slovaks turning hard work into success. Joseph Hornak (seated, right), a steelworker, and his wife Maria (seated, left) saw to it that their children were properly educated. Two of their daughters, Veronica (standing, second from the left) and Helen (seated, second from the left) would go on to become sisters of Notre Dame. Veronica and her parents were born in Krakovany, now in Slovakia in historic Nitra County. Also shown here is Joseph (center) sitting next to Emil. Standing in the back row are Anna (left), Marie (third from the left), and Michael (right). (Courtesy of Joseph Hornack.)

The Tindira family from what is now Brezovica, Slovakia, arrived in America to work in lead mines in Missouri. When they moved to Cleveland, one branch settled on the southeast side, while others settled in the Tremont area, depending on where they found jobs. Shown here is the 1906 wedding of John Tindira and Mary Krupa. Old country ties were strong, and the woman on the right, Veronica Tindira, would later marry Steve Heredos (seated left) who was also from Brezovica. The young girl in front is Anne, John and Veronica's sister. (Courtesy of Raymond Tindira.)

Julia Tindira (making her First Holy Communion) and brother Andrew are shown around 1920. The veil that Julia is wearing, however, is not the veil she started with that day. As she walked into the church, she passed under an arch near some lighted candles, and her original veil caught fire. One of the sisters put out the fire, but not before the veil was ruined. Luckily, the sister had a spare, which Julia wore for the rest of the day. (Courtesy of Raymond Tindira.)

Ferdinand Ungvarsky, a founding member of Nativity of the Blessed Virgin Mary (BVM) parish, immigrated to the United States from what is now Uzovský Šalgov, Slovakia. Shown here in 1912, he served as the church custodian during its early years. He is shown cutting the high grass on the parish property on Dunlap Avenue. (Courtesy of the Slovak Institute and Library.)

Frank Rossy and Veronica Jurcak, shown on the right in their wedding picture from 1915, were both children of Slovak parents from the southeast side—Frank coming from St. Ladislas Church, and Veronica from Nativity BVM parish. They eventually settled near East (now Martin Luther King Jr.) Boulevard in an area that would eventually become part of St. Benedict parish, raising a daughter and two sons. (Courtesy of James Virost.)

Two

FOR GOD AND COUNTRY
PART I

Fr. Stefan Furdek is considered a prime mover and organizer among Slovaks in the United States. Following his arrival in Cleveland to be pastor of Our Lady of Lourdes Church, he went on to establish St. Ladislas parish and the First Catholic Slovak Union and to assist in founding the First Catholic Slovak Ladies Association. A tireless worker for Slovak and Czech causes, he died in 1915. (Courtesy of Our Lady of Lourdes Parish.)

Although Slovaks began arriving in Cleveland around 1880, it was difficult to find Slovak-speaking priests. So it was not until 1885 that the Cleveland Catholic Diocese could establish a parish to serve them. Their first parish was St. Ladislas, which eventually built a church at Corwin (East 92nd) Street and Holton Avenue. Early parishioners shared the facility with Cleveland's Hungarian community, but because of bitter feelings between the two groups, a split was ordered. The Slovaks kept the St. Ladislas property after paying the Hungarians, who established their own church—St. Elizabeth—on Buckeye Road. (Courtesy of the Slovak Institute and Library.)

As originally built, the second church building of St. Ladislas parish had a tall steeple, not the truncated tower that many remember. Over the years, age and the elements had taken their toll, and the steeple was eventually removed. (Courtesy of Ronald Seman.)

16

From 1885 to 1971, St. Ladislas parish was considered the mother church of Cleveland Slovaks. Founded in 1885 by Fr. Stefan Furdek, St. Ladislas is considered linked to all of Cleveland's Slovak Catholic parishes. From its founding, the community worshipped in a number of other spaces until it was permanently established in 1889 at East 92nd Street and Holton Avenue. This building, dedicated in 1906, would serve generations of Cleveland Slovaks before it was destroyed by fire in 1970. (Courtesy of Archives, Diocese of Cleveland.)

This scene of the interior of St. Ladislas Church is probably from a parish anniversary celebration. The canopy to the left indicates that the bishop of Cleveland was present for the celebration. (Courtesy of Ronald Seman.)

On August 8, 1970, fire of unknown origin destroyed the St. Ladislas Church building. With the parish population down to about 100 families, members of Cleveland's first Slovak Roman Catholic parish continued to attend mass in the school auditorium. Finally in November 1971, the parish was officially closed. (Courtesy of Ronald Seman.)

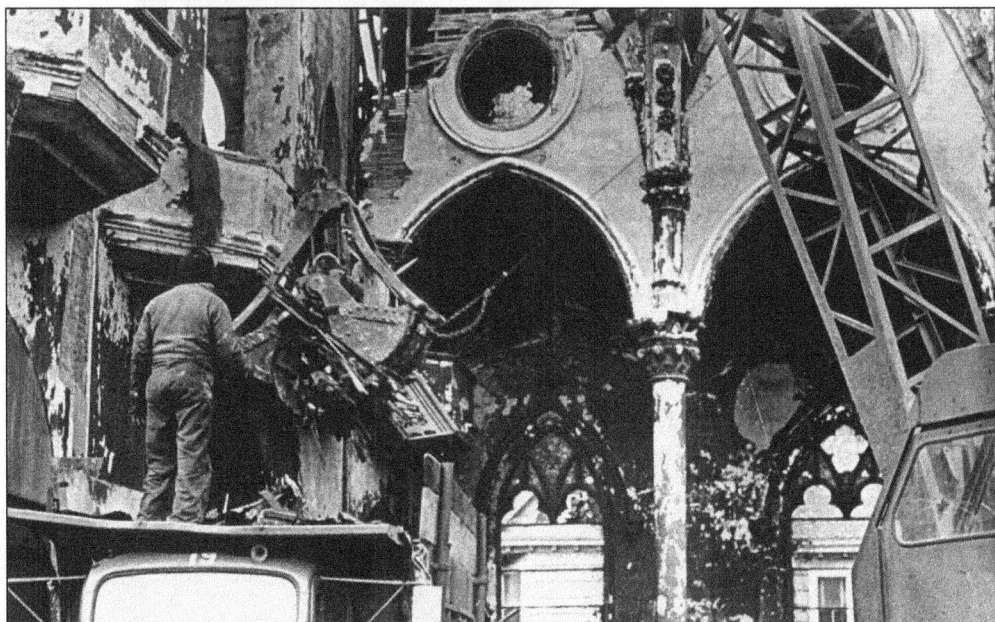

Wrecking crews tear apart the insides of St. Ladislas Church in August 1970, shortly after the church was destroyed by fire. Amid this destruction, one stained-glass window was discovered intact. This window would become part of a new St. Ladislas Church that was built in the Cleveland suburb of Westlake. The new church has no connection to Cleveland's Slovak community. (Courtesy of Ronald Seman.)

Holy Trinity Slovak Lutheran Church has its roots in Cleveland's Slovak Lutheran community, which started to form around 1890. After some difficult formative years, Holy Trinity became Cleveland's first Slovak Lutheran congregation, establishing itself on Woodland Avenue, near Harmon (East 20th) Street. The congregation later moved to East 20th Street north of Woodland, building this church in 1906. In the late 1950s, the church building was taken for Cleveland's Innerbelt Freeway, and the congregation dedicated a new church on Broadview Road in Parma in 1960. An early leader in Holy Trinity's community was the noted Cleveland Slovak Jan Pankuch. (Courtesy of the Cleveland Press Archives—Cleveland State University Library Special Collections.)

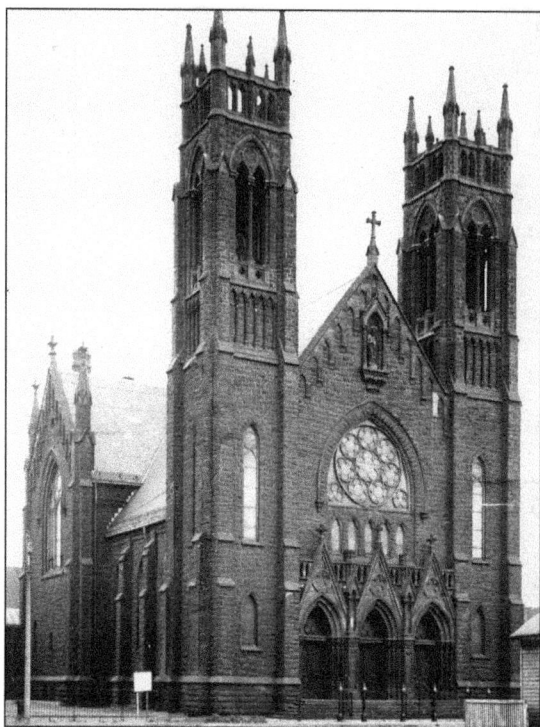

The next Slovak Catholic parish to be established after St. Ladislas was St. Martin's at Chapel (East 23rd) Street and Scovill Avenue in 1893. The establishment of this parish only eight years after St. Ladislas was founded is evidence of how fast the Slovak immigrant community was growing. This building, dedicated in 1907, could hold 1,000 worshippers. (Courtesy of Archives, Diocese of Cleveland.)

The interior of the Gothic St. Martin's Church is shown in this undated photograph. The canopy on the left indicates the bishop of Cleveland was present for this celebration. The parish included a school that at one time numbered 1,000 pupils. The St. Martin's neighborhood in Cleveland's central city changed rapidly, and the parish closed in September 1960, a victim of urban population changes and the growth of Cleveland's freeway system. (Courtesy of Archives, Diocese of Cleveland.)

SS. Peter and Paul Evangelical Lutheran Church, 13030 Madison Avenue in Lakewood, was established in 1901 to serve Slovak Lutherans residing in that community. The first church was built at Thrush and Quail Avenues, where services were held until 1927, when this building was dedicated. Noted Cleveland Slovak leader Jan Pankuch was a founding member of this church. (Courtesy of the Cleveland Press Archives—Cleveland State University Library Special Collections.)

This is the interior of SS. Peter and Paul Evangelical Lutheran Church in Lakewood, shown in 1952. The congregation, established in 1901, built this church in 1926 for $143,000. Two other Lutheran congregations in Lakewood that broke off from SS. Peter and Paul are Pentecost Lutheran and Gethsemane Lutheran. In 2003, Pentecost and SS. Peter and Paul merged to form a new congregation at this site, Grace Lutheran. (Courtesy of the Cleveland Press Archives— Cleveland State University Library Special Collections.)

The cornerstone of SS. Peter and Paul Evangelical Lutheran Church in Lakewood carries an inscription in Slovak. From 1901 to 1935, services were conducted primarily in Slovak. In 1935, it was decided to conduct some services and classes in English to keep the church's younger generation intact. (Courtesy of the Cleveland Press Archives— Cleveland State University Library Special Collections.)

Slovaks started to settle in the eastern end of Lakewood, particularly along Madison Avenue, around 1892, when the National Carbon Company (later Union Carbide, now GrafTech International) built its plant on Madison and West 117th Street. Slovak Catholics were still attending mass at St. Ladislas Church, almost 11 miles away, and in 1903, they received permission to establish the parish of SS. Cyril and Methodius on land purchased near Madison and Lakewood Avenue. This combination church and school was built in 1905 and is identical to the first church built by Nativity BVM Slovak parish. (Courtesy of the Slovak Institute and Library.)

SS. Cyril and Methodius Church was housed in another combination church and school building from 1916 until the current church structure was completed in 1931. This building, shown in 1971, was completed at a cost of $228,000. Much of the interior decoration, including murals, was designed and executed by Jozef Cincik, noted Slovak artist and cofounder of the Slovak Institute at St. Andrew Svorad Abbey. (Courtesy of the Cleveland Press Archives—Cleveland State University Library Special Collections.)

The interior of SS. Cyril and Methodius Church is shown in 1966 on the 50th anniversary of the ordination of its pastor, Msgr. Francis Dubosh. (Courtesy of the Slovak Institute and Library.)

Msgr. Francis Dubosh served from 1927 to 1967 as the fourth pastor of SS. Cyril and Methodius parish. Besides leading the parish and supervising major building programs—including the current church in 1931—he also supported the freedom of Slovaks in Europe. He was also instrumental in founding the Slovak Radio Club in 1938. A weekly radio program sponsored by the club continues in Cleveland to this day. (Courtesy of the Slovak Institute and Library.)

Still standing into the 21st century is the original church structure of SS. Cyril and Methodius Church on Lakewood Avenue. This church was built in 1905 as a combination church and school, with the school on the first floor and the church on the second floor. In 1978, it was still being used for meetings and as a gymnasium. (Courtesy of the Cleveland Press Archives—Cleveland State University Library Special Collections.)

If this building seems familiar, it is because the first church structure of Nativity BVM parish is indeed identical to the first church built by SS. Cyril and Methodius Church in Lakewood. Both parishes were established in 1903, with Nativity parishioners buying lots on Aetna Road near Woodland Hills Avenue (East 93rd Street). Slovaks had been settling in that area, close to the Newburgh Works of American Steel and Wire Company, shortly before 1900 and attending services at St. Ladislas Church, more than two miles away. After obtaining permission to establish a parish, they chose the name SS. Cyril and Methodius, only to learn that Lakewood Slovaks had beaten them to that name. They chose instead the name Nativity of the Blessed Virgin Mary. (Courtesy of Archives, Diocese of Cleveland.)

Fr. Vaclav Chaloupka was the fifth pastor of Nativity BVM Church, although many parishioners regarded him as the founding pastor. A Czech by birth, he came in 1908 to the Slovak parish, which was founded in 1903. He is shown in his rectory office—sometime between 1910 and 1914. Father Chaloupka died in 1956. (Courtesy of the Slovak Institute and Library.)

By 1925, Nativity BVM parish had far outgrown its original church/school structure, and plans were laid for a new church building. With parishioners selling individual bricks for this building, initial funds were raised and the cornerstone was laid in July 1925. The structure, built largely through the labor of Nativity parishioners, opened in October 1927. (Courtesy of John T. Sabol.)

St. Wendelin Church on Columbus Road in Cleveland sits within a combination church-school building. Construction for this building began in 1924 and was finished in late 1925 at a cost of $240,000. Twelve years later, the Slovak parish built a hall and gymnasium at a cost of $37,000. The debts from both of these buildings were paid off by July 1943. In 2009, the Cleveland Catholic Diocese designated St. Wendelin parish to be closed. (Courtesy of the Anniversary Publications Company, Cleveland.)

St. Wendelin parish on Columbus Road was one of three parishes established in 1903 to serve Cleveland's rapidly growing Slovak community. After a succession of three pastors during its first five years, Fr. (later Msgr.) Augustin Tomasek became pastor in 1908, serving until 1957. This was a period of tremendous growth for the parish, including a new school, church, and parish hall to meet the needs of Slovaks, who were arriving in the area, and their growing families. (Courtesy of St. Wendelin Church.)

Msgr. Augustin Tomasek was still pastor when he celebrated his 50th anniversary as a priest in 1955. Shown here are the cadets of the First Catholic Slovak Ladies Association, who were on hand for this celebration. Monsignor Tomasek died in 1957. (Courtesy of St. Wendelin Church.)

St. Andrew parish on East 51st Street and Superior Avenue was established in 1906 to serve Slovaks working and living in the north-central area of Cleveland. The founding pastor was Fr. Emil Sloupsky, who quickly set about to build a church and establish a school. The parish grew rapidly, and in 1908, Fr. John Liscinsky was appointed as second pastor. In 1922, at the urging of the Slovak Catholic Federation, the Cleveland Catholic Diocese invited Benedictine monks from Lisle, Illinois, to establish a community in Cleveland. St. Andrew's was chosen as the site, and after the monks arrived, work began on the second church, shown here in 1927—about a year after the church was dedicated. (Courtesy of St. Andrew Svorad Abbey.)

St. Andrew Church had Spanish mission–style architecture, as shown by the church's bells in this 1961 photograph. The parish was the first location for Benedictine High School, opened in 1927 with 35 students. With the gradual movement of most of its parishioners to the suburbs and elsewhere, the parish closed in 2008 and the church was demolished in 2009. (Courtesy of the Cleveland Press Archives—Cleveland State University Library Special Collections.)

Dr. Martin Luther Evangelical Lutheran Church was established in 1910 to serve Slovak Lutherans who had been increasing in number in Cleveland's south side (Tremont). After worshipping in a two-story home on West 14th Street for five years, the congregation decided to build at this site in 1915. This structure, at 2139 West 14th Street, was dedicated in 1917. The congregation later moved to Ridge Road in Brooklyn, where a church was built and dedicated in 1958. (Courtesy of the Cleveland Press Archives—Cleveland State University Library Special Collections.)

Pentecost Evangelical Lutheran Church, at 13303 Madison Avenue in Lakewood, was established in 1918 after its founding members had broken off from SS. Peter and Paul Lutheran Church. This 1968 photograph shows a wing built at that time. (Courtesy of the Cleveland Press Archives— Cleveland State University Library Special Collections.)

This is the interior of Pentecost Evangelical Lutheran Church in Lakewood at the time of its 50th anniversary in 1968. In 2003, Pentecost and SS. Peter and Paul merged to form a new congregation at this site, Grace Lutheran. (Courtesy of the Cleveland Press Archives—Cleveland State University Library Special Collections.)

The original church and houses of Our Lady of Mercy Parish on West 11th Street in Cleveland's Tremont area are shown in 1926. The parish, originally named St. John the Baptist Church, was established in 1917 as a Polish National Catholic parish belonging to the Polish National Catholic Diocese of Scranton. After the death of Cleveland Catholic bishop John Farrelly, who had refused to establish a Roman Catholic parish for Slovaks in Tremont, parishioners petitioned his successor, Bishop Joseph Schrembs, who agreed to reestablish the parish as Roman Catholic. (Courtesy of Our Lady of Mercy Church.)

The choir of St. John the Baptist Church, predecessor of Our Lady of Mercy, is shown in 1918. St. John the Baptist was formed in 1917 after Catholics in Tremont were rebuffed by Cleveland Roman Catholic bishop John Farrelly, when they asked the diocese to establish a Roman Catholic parish near their homes. (Courtesy of Jim Noga.)

This is the interior of the original church of Our Lady of Mercy parish and would also have been the interior of St. John the Baptist Church. Shown here at the wedding of Betty and Michael Kuchta in 1944, the church would be demolished in 1948 when the present church was built. (Courtesy of Jim Noga.)

Following World War II, Our Lady of Mercy parish finally began to build a new church at a cost of $157,000. Fr. James Slaminka, associate pastor, assisted in the groundbreaking for the new church, planned to seat 500 worshippers, in May 1948. The church was completed by October 1949. (Courtesy of Our Lady of Mercy Church.)

In 1942, Our Lady of Mercy parishioners began a pledge campaign to raise money for a new church. Although $51,000 was raised that year, construction was delayed until the end of World War II. The modern Romanesque-style church rises to a height of 56 feet. The bell is from the original church. In 2009, the Cleveland Catholic Diocese designated Our Lady of Mercy to be closed. (Courtesy of Our Lady of Mercy Church.)

The interior of Our Lady of Mercy has a Slovak motif, with many of the designs taken from peasant decorations. According to the parish's 75th anniversary history, "a ribbon effect flows like peasants in dance with free-flowing design that might be on the dress of a man or woman." Even the colors used are true to Slovak costumes and designs. (Courtesy of Our Lady of Mercy Church.)

After establishing itself on East 51st Street and Superior Avenue, the St. Andrew Svorad Priory (later St. Andrew Svorad Abbey) and Benedictine High School moved farther east in 1929, purchasing St. Mary's Institute for Girls run by the Sisters of Notre Dame on Buckeye Road. This building is one of the original structures of the abbey and the high school at its present site. (Photograph by Gus Fretter, courtesy of the Cleveland Press Archives—Cleveland State University Library Special Collections.)

St. Andrew Abbey Church was built as part of a major renovation of St. Andrew Svorad Abbey in the 1980s. The church, which replaced a basement chapel, was made possible by a donation from the First Catholic Slovak Ladies Association. This expansion and renovation of the abbey and Benedictine High School reaffirmed the commitment of the Slovak Benedictines to the city and to their continuing contribution to stability within this area. (Courtesy of St. Andrew Svorad Abbey.)

In 1928, the Cleveland Catholic Diocese split the St. Ladislas Slovak congregation, establishing St. Benedict parish at East (now Martin Luther King Jr.) Boulevard and Lamontier Avenue. Although staffed by Benedictine monks, the parish is not named for the order's founder but for St. Benedict of Skalka, a Slovak saint and the student of St. Andrew Svorad, for whom St. Andrew abbey and parish are named. The original church shown here was built as part of the St. Benedict School. (Courtesy of Jan Zamiska.)

The original St. Benedict Church was contained inside the school building, a style also used by St. Wendelin Church on the west side. A crowd fills the church here in the late 1940s—possibly for the installation of Abbot Theodore Kojis, OSB, in 1946. (Courtesy of St. Andrew Svorad Abbey.)

In June 1946, the monks of St. Andrew Svorad Abbey elected Fr. Theodore Kojis as their second abbot, succeeding Abbot Stanislaus Gmuca. Members of the St. Andrew Benedictine community at that time are, from left to right, (first row) Father Gilbert, Father Wendelin, Father Ivan, Father Charles, Father Leo, Father Celestine, Fr. George Luba, prior, Abbot President Mark Braun (not a member of the St. Andrew Benedictine community), Abbot Theodore Kojis, Father Paul, Father Michael, Father John, Father Sylvester, Father Daniel, Father Armand, and Father Stephen; (second row) Father Bartholomew, Father Placid, Father Peter, Father Dominic, Brother Martin, Brother Nicholas, Father Maurus, Father Aloysius, Brother Martin, Father

Method, Father Benedict, Father Cyril, Brother Benedict, Father Philip, Father Andrew, Father Augustine, Father Mark, and Father Thomas; (third row) Father Luke, Father Florian, Father Louis, Father Martin, Father Gilbert, Father Robert, Brother Anthony, Father Matthew, Brother Florian, Brother Method, Father Francis, and Father Edward; (fourth row) Brother Laurence, Father Gregory, Father Bernard, Brother Aloysius, Father David, Father James, Father Raphael, Father Joseph, and Father Jerome (who would become the community's third abbot). (Courtesy of St. Andrew Svorad Abbey.)

Servers from the seventh and eighth grades as well as high school servers from St. Benedict Church pose with Fr. Joseph Karaba, OSB, assistant pastor in 1945 or 1946. From left to right are (first row) Joseph Mitchell, John Knuth, Joseph Stipkala, and Clarence Franko; (second row) Chuck Sabatos, John Miklus, Andy Konkoly, Richard Homrocky, Ray Ponchak, Bob David, Steve Yurko, John Papson, Thomas Laczko, and Al Onchak; (third row) Don Pillar, Don Sabovik, Anthony Stefanek, Bob Yurcisin, Steve Skunta, Jim Hovan, James St. John, and Edward Wilkes; (fourth row) Bob Puzder, John Kolenich, Roland Horvath, unidentified, Benedict Palsa, Joe Hornack, Jack St. John, Bob Malinak, and Frank Stipkala; (fifth row) Jim Zeleznik, Ed Kozma, Gerald Markus, Jim Kvoriak, Stephen Placko, Rudy Janecek, Bill Sopko, George Dachtler, and Richard Markus. (Courtesy of the Slovak Institute and Library.)

Shown here is the final structure of St. Benedict Church shortly before construction was completed in 1953. The school, which contained the former church, stands behind this building and continued to serve the parish until the parish closed in 1993. (Courtesy of the Cleveland Press Archives—Cleveland State University Library Special Collections.)

This photograph, believed to be from the 25th anniversary of St. Benedict Church, coincides with the opening of this new structure in 1953. The church's interior contained nine marble altars and had a seating capacity of 1,300. It was regarded as one of the largest Slovak Catholic churches in the United States. (Courtesy of St. Andrew Abbey.)

The Vincentian Sisters of Charity arrived in Bedford on September 4, 1928, at the invitation of Archbishop Joseph Schrembs to minister to Cleveland's Slovak immigrants. The community established the Shrine of Our Lady of Levocha in 1930. (Courtesy of the Sisters of Charity of Cincinnati.)

The first three women to enter the Vincentian community in Bedford are, from left to right, Sr. M. Bernarda Arway, Sr. M. Bonaventure, and Sr. M. Joseph Slavik. They are shown on their reception day, April 24, 1929. (Courtesy of the Slovak Institute and Library.)

The outdoor Shrine of Our Lady of Levocha (shown under construction) provides for visitors during the summer months and is a location for numerous liturgies related to important events in Slovak history. (Courtesy of the Sisters of Charity of Cincinnati.)

The Shrine of Our Lady of Levocha is named for the city of Levoca in historic Spis County of Slovakia, a center for Catholic pilgrimages. In 2003, the Vincentian Sisters of Charity merged with the Sisters of Charity of Cincinnati. Besides teaching work, the Vincentians also served in hospitals and ministered to the poor in Greater Cleveland and elsewhere throughout the United States and in El Salvador. (Courtesy of the Sisters of Charity of Cincinnati.)

Shown here is the altar at the Shrine of Our Lady of Levocha in Bedford. The Vincentian Sisters of Charity have served as teachers in 18 schools in the Cleveland Catholic Diocese, including Lumen Cordium High School, which was established on the community's property in 1963 and closed in 1987. (Courtesy of the Sisters of Charity of Cincinnati.)

The Shrine of Our Lady of Levocha sits on the grounds of the motherhouse of the Slovak Vincentian Sisters of Charity in Bedford. Each year a Slovak festival and picnic would also include mass, a procession that passed by statues on the grounds, ethnic food, and ethnic folk dancing. (Courtesy of Eileen Sotak.)

Three

FOR THE GOOD OF ALL

Cleveland is the site of the founding of the First Catholic Slovak Union, one of the largest Slovak fraternal organizations in the United States. In September 1890, these men met at the request of Rev. Stefan Furdek to establish the society to help members deepen their religious faith and require them to become U.S. citizens. It also established an insurance fund, published the weekly newspaper *Jednota*, and, as a cultural organization, protected the Slovak language and heritage. Shown here are the society's founders in 1890. From left to right are (first row) Martin Slanina, Rev. Jan Martvon (pastor of St. Ladislas Church), Rev. Ervin Gelhoff (Streator, Illinois), Father Furdek, and Juraj Onda; (second row) Andrej Benovic, J. A. Filek, Jan Brehovic, J. Prokopovic, J. Bakos, Andrej Sotak, and Jakub Gruss, credited as being the first Slovak in Cleveland. (Courtesy of the Slovak Institute and Library.)

Juraj Onda, first president of the First Catholic Slovak Union, took that office after the society's founder, Rev. Stefan Furdek, refused the presidency. A carpenter, Onda arrived in the United States in 1888. (Courtesy of the Slovak Institute and Library.)

The First Catholic Slovak Union (later known as the First Catholic Slovak Union of the USA and Canada) was founded in 1890 and grew to more than 50,000 members by 1918. By 1933, the organization established its national headquarters at 3289 East 55th Street, near Broadway. This building served until the group purchased a larger corporate headquarters at 6611 Rockside Road, Independence, in 1995. (Courtesy of the Cleveland Press Archives—Cleveland State University Library Special Collections.)

In 1892, Anna Hurban, a 35-year-old Slovak mother from Gbely in Nitra County, began to lay the groundwork for one of the largest Slovak fraternal organizations in the United States. Concerned that Slovak women and children needed the same insurance protection as their husbands (already insured through the First Catholic Slovak Union), Hurban and eight other Slovak women met on January 1, 1892, to establish the First Catholic Slovak Ladies Association. Rev. Stefan Furdek, First Catholic Slovak Union founder, encouraged the women in their effort. (Courtesy of the Slovak Institute and Library.)

For the first 38 years of its existence, the First Catholic Slovak Ladies Association was headquartered in private homes. In 1929, the association broke ground for this building on Lee Road in Shaker Heights, which was completed and opened by July 1930. (Courtesy of the Cleveland Press Archives—Cleveland State University Library Special Collections.)

Cadets of a Slovak fraternal organization assembled for this early photograph outside the original structure of SS. Cyril and Methodius Church in Lakewood. Third from the right in the third row is Method Likavec, who immigrated to the United States in 1902 and worked as a machinist at the National Carbon Company. Many others in this group would have also worked there. (Courtesy of Louise O'Boyle.)

Decked out in their new uniforms, the cadets of the St. George Society, Branch 14 of the First Catholic Slovak Union, pose in front of St. Ladislas Church in October 1906. (Courtesy of the Slovak Institute and Library.)

Cadets of the First Catholic Slovak Union march in downtown Cleveland in August 1927. These cadets performed and served at many civic and religious functions. (Courtesy of the Cleveland Press Archives—Cleveland State University Library Special Collections.)

The First Catholic Slovak Ladies Association grew rapidly in its early years. From 1893 to 1915, assets grew an average of 86 percent every two years. Illustrating that growth is this photograph of the Our Lady of Levocha Lodge of the First Catholic Slovak Ladies Association at St. Wendelin Church in May 1910. At the time this photograph was taken St. Wendelin parish was only seven years old. (Courtesy of St. Wendelin Church.)

Cadets of the First Catholic Slovak Ladies Association parade at Cleveland Stadium on September 4, 1934, as part of the triennial convention of the First Catholic Slovak Union. Delegates to the convention heard a speech by Archbishop Joseph Schrembs of the

Cleveland Catholic Diocese, who made an appeal for labor peace in an address at St. John Cathedral. (Courtesy of the Cleveland Press Archives—Cleveland State University Library Special Collections.)

First Catholic Slovak Ladies Association Branch 141 marked its 50th anniversary and the 50th anniversary of Nativity BVM parish in 1953. Shown from left to right are (first row) Veronica Skladany, Anna Bednar, Teresa Chovancek, Maria Jurcak (founder of Branch 141), Susan Matuscak (national financial secretary), Anna Yasso (national treasurer), and Mary Pencak; (second row) Tillie Bacik, Mary Kraft, Frances Misenko (secretary of the First Catholic Slovak Ladies Association Junior Order), and Elizabeth Spisak. (Courtesy of Joan Thesling.)

In 1906, Cleveland Slovaks broke ground for a Slovak National Home (Narodny Slovensky Dom) to be built at 8804 Buckeye Road. Sadly, as Eleanor Ledbetter recounts in her 1918 book *Slovaks in Cleveland*, "its management has unfortunately not been entirely successful, and its ownership is now vested in M.N. Soboslay . . . who regards it as held in trust for its original purposes." (Courtesy of the Slovak Institute and Library.)

Four

SCHOOL DAYS
SLOVAK STYLE

With the rush of Slovak immigrants up to 1924, many Slovak Catholic parishes were also rushing to accommodate their needs. Crowded classes such as this second grade from St. Wendelin School in 1922 were not unusual. After holding classes in the St. Wendelin convent, the parish built a brick school in 1905. Included in this photograph is Steve Sotak (first row, third from the left), whose father, John, arrived in the United States from Nižný Hrušov in historic Zemplin County in the early 1900s. (Courtesy of Eileen Sotak.)

St. Ladislas parish established a school during its early years, with classes conducted in the church. Classes later moved to a frame building, then to this brick structure on the church property on Holton Avenue. It is believed this photograph was taken in 1918. (Courtesy of Archives, Diocese of Cleveland.)

In 1923, St. Ladislas purchased land on Lamontier Avenue near East (now Martin Luther King Jr.) Boulevard, several blocks east of the parish property, and built this school for $250,000. The building would later become St. Benedict Skalka Church and school. (Courtesy of the Slovak Institute and Library.)

These "Dutch girls" are dressed for their parts in a play, which would have been presented as part of the Nativity BVM school graduation ceremonies sometime in the early 1920s. It was expected that each class would present a short sketch as part of the evening's festivities. This tradition continued until the death of Pastor Fr. Vaclav Chaloupka in 1956. (Courtesy of the Slovak Institute and Library.)

Nativity BVM school on Aetna Road was built on the site of the original church, which was moved to the next street south, Dunlap Avenue, around 1915. The school was built in stages beginning in 1916, with an east wing (left) built in 1924 and the west wing built in 1930. At one time, almost 1,000 children attended the school's eight grades. (Courtesy of Archives, Diocese of Cleveland.)

Nativity BVM parish and school grew quickly in its early years, and graduating classes increased in size each year. The class of 1917 was the eighth class to graduate. Most of the boys went directly into nearby mills or other factories. If a family could afford it, they would send a son or daughter to a Catholic high school. Often, however, it was necessary for a son or daughter to go to work to help support the family. (Courtesy of Archives, Diocese of Cleveland.)

By 1924, Nativity BVM school on Aetna Road was quickly expanding with the addition of an east wing. The original church—formerly on Aetna Road, where the school stands—is shown in the background facing Dunlap Avenue, the first street south of Aetna. Nativity's second church would not be built for about 10 more years. (Courtesy of the Slovak Institute and Library.)

Our Lady of Mercy School was built in 1926 to replace a three-room frame school. Originally staffed by the Sisters of Notre Dame, from 1935 the school was staffed by Vincentian Sisters of Charity from Cleveland. In 1947, a kindergarten was established. This is a seventh-grade classroom from the 1940s. (Courtesy of Our Lady of Mercy Church.)

Slovak children at Nativity BVM school are shown in this classroom scene from the 1930s. On the blackboard is part of a religion lesson, including a chalk drawing of the interior of Nativity BVM Church. School construction started in 1916 and proceeded in stages until completion in 1930. (Courtesy of Mary Ann Hisnay.)

In 1953, St. Wendelin Parish celebrated its 50th anniversary. As part of the celebration, the parish honored the Sisters of Notre Dame and Vincentian Sisters of Charity who taught in the parish school. The Vincentians are a primarily Slovak order that have recently merged with the Sisters of Charity of Cincinnati. (Courtesy of St. Wendelin Church.)

Children at St. Wendelin School were also taught by Vincentian Sisters of Charity located in Bedford. Shown here are St. Wendelin parishioners who went on to join this order. (Courtesy of St. Wendelin Church.)

Sisters of Notre Dame originally taught children at St. Wendelin School. Shown in this photograph from the parish's 50th anniversary in 1953 are St. Wendelin parishioners who joined that order. They are, from left to right, (first row) Sisters Veronica, Robert, Valerie, and Wendelin; (second row) Sisters Annelle, Ludmilla, Michaelene, Deana, Robertine, and Theodore. (Courtesy of St. Wendelin Church.)

As many as three generations of parishioners at Nativity BVM school knew Sister Anastasia, who taught there and for seven years at St. John Nepomucene Czech Catholic School. She joined the Adrian Dominican order at a young age and taught at the Nativity school as early as 1912. Fluent in Slovak, she also spent a great deal of time teaching English to immigrant children. (Courtesy of John Hopko.)

This is the entire student body and faculty of Benedictine High School, which opened in 1927 at the site of St. Andrew parish on Superior Avenue. Seated at the lower right is Julius Badzik, the first lay teacher on the Benedictine faculty. A Slovak whose family came from Hrabusice in historic Spis County, he came to the United States as a child in 1903. He taught Latin, history, and civics and, as a practicing attorney, assisted the school in obtaining the real estate for its current location. He also provided significant assistance in raising funds to purchase the property. (Courtesy of the Slovak Institute and Library.)

Benedictine High School on Martin Luther King Jr. Boulevard, south of Buckeye Road, traces its origins to Slovak Benedictine monks who arrived in Cleveland in 1922. The school, established to educate Slovak young men, opened its doors in 1927. This building was erected in 1940. (Courtesy of St. Andrew Abbey.)

Benedictine High School, which is today a college preparatory school, sought to reach a wider spectrum in its early days. With a focus on educating Slovak young men to make their mark in society, the school offered a wide range of course offerings, including these shop classes. (Courtesy of St. Andrew Abbey.)

From 1955 to 1994 Augie Bossu (center) coached hundreds of young men at Benedictine High School, earning him the title of Ohio's winningest high school football coach. He led his players to 14 city championship appearances, winning nine and tying two. His teams recorded 310 wins, 130 losses, and 20 ties. Before coming to Benedictine, Bossu spent seven years at two other high schools. (Courtesy of St. Andrew Abbey.)

Before Bossu took the helm as Benedictine High School football coach, Joe Rufus coached the team to several winning seasons, which included this 26-18 victory over St. Ignatius High School in the 1952 city championship game. More than 33,000 fans at Cleveland Stadium watched this Thanksgiving Day game. Shown on the right is Benedictine player Bill Gries, later Bishop Roger Gries, OSB, auxiliary bishop of Cleveland. (Courtesy of the Cleveland Press Archives—Cleveland State University Library Special Collections.)

Five

FOR GOD AND COUNTRY
PART II

Most Slovaks sought U.S. citizenship as soon as possible after arriving from Europe and establishing their families here. Churches conducted English and citizenship classes for these new arrivals. The National Carbon Company (later Union Carbide, now GrafTech International) in Lakewood also conducted citizenship classes and encouraged Slovak immigrants to seek naturalization. (Courtesy of the Lakewood Historical Society.)

Shown here is the crowd that gathered at Cleveland's Gray's Armory on May 26, 1907, for the founding of the Slovak League of America. The Slovak League was born in response to the need to bring into worldview the political and social plight of the Slovak nation, then a part of the Austro-Hungarian Empire. It was the prime mover behind what is known as the Cleveland Agreement in 1915, which brought a pledge of equality for Czechs and Slovaks in any new state to be created at the end of World War I. Newspapers at the time estimated the crowd here at about 7,000, including Slovaks and Rusyns. (Courtesy of the Slovak Institute and Library.)

This photograph of Cleveland's Slovak and Czech legionnaires was taken at an unknown location sometime before America's entry into World War I. A total of 360 Slovak and Czech volunteers from Cleveland joined other Slovaks and Czechs from the United States and abroad to create the Czechoslovak Legion in Europe, fighting against the Austro-Hungarian Empire for the ultimate independence of their homeland. Cleveland Slovaks also donated more than $10,000 to this cause, according to Jan Pankuch in his book *The History of Slovaks of Cleveland and Lakewood*. (Courtesy of the Slovak Institute and Library.)

This is part of the crowd of Cleveland Slovaks and Czechs that gathered at the Cleveland Music Hall on October 11, 1938, about a week and a half following the German invasion of Czechoslovakia. Both the Slovak and Czech communities were concerned about the invasion, which would eventually result in the Nazi occupation of Bohemia and the establishment of the Slovak Republic in 1939. (Courtesy of the Cleveland Press Archives—Cleveland State University Library Special Collections.)

Dressed in *kroje* from their various ancestral villages, Slovak and Czech women parade on Clark Avenue on September 4, 1940, to mark the anniversary of the establishment of the Czechoslovak republic in 1918. This parade had special significance because of the Nazi invasion of Czechoslovakia in 1938. (Courtesy of the Cleveland Press Archives—Cleveland State University Library Special Collections.)

In 1931, a group of veterans who saw service as volunteers under Gen. Milan Stefanik during World War I founded Camp Bradlo in Richfield. Stefanik, Tomas Masaryk, and Eduard Benes are regarded as the founders of Czechoslovakia in 1918. Shown here in a 1941 photograph are, from left to right, Stephen Amrich, Walter Zevchik, and George Simon preparing a special barbecue roast at the camp. (Courtesy of the Cleveland Public Library, Photograph Collection.)

Camp Bradlo in Richfield, named for Mount Bradlo in present-day Slovakia, where Gen. Milan Stefanik is buried, comprises 90 acres, including a pavilion and other recreational facilities. Shown here is the Kitchen Committee at Camp Bradlo. (Courtesy of the Cleveland Public Library, Photograph Collection.)

Each May 4, Cleveland Slovaks gather at the statue of Gen. Milan Stefanik at the western edge of University Circle to mark the date of his death. Shown here in 1934, on the 15th anniversary of that event, is one of the pioneers of Greater Cleveland's Slovak community, Jan Pankuch (center). Holding wreaths are Joseph V. Skarupa and Julius Slavsky. Pankuch was a signer of the Cleveland and Pittsburgh Agreements, which laid the groundwork for establishing the country of Czechoslovakia. A former president of the National Slovak Society, he was the author of the definitive history of the early Slovaks in the area, *History of the Slovaks of Cleveland and Lakewood*, originally written in Slovak in 1930 and translated into English in 2001 through the collaboration of Joseph Hornack of the Slovak Institute and Library and Rasto Gallo. (Courtesy of the Cleveland Press Archives—Cleveland State University Library Special Collections.)

Cleveland Slovaks supported America's efforts in World War II. Signing up for stamps and war bonds in September 1942 are John Kanuck and Joseph Prussa, representing the Slovak Catholic Sokols from Passaic, New Jersey. At the table are Suzanne Buynak and Anna Voytko of Cleveland. Standing on the right is the national president of the Slovak Catholic Sokols, Dominic Sloboda of Lorain. (Courtesy of the Cleveland Press Archives—Cleveland State University Library Special Collections.)

In a march down Euclid Avenue at East 17th Street, Cleveland Slovaks joined with other Slavic groups in Cleveland in 1942 to support fellow Slavs under Nazi oppression in Europe. (Courtesy of Robert Hlasko.)

More than 674 men and women from St. Wendelin parish served in U.S. armed forces during World War II. To honor those individuals, the parish proudly displayed this honor roll of those who were serving. (Courtesy of St. Wendelin Church.)

For many years, Cleveland Slovaks and Czechs carried bitter memories of the Russian invasion of their country on August 21, 1968. This demonstration on August 27, 1971, protested the tragic events of 1968. (Courtesy of the Cleveland Press Archives— Cleveland State University Library Special Collections.)

The *Post* was published by Post 381 of the Catholic War Veterans. Begun in 1938, the newspaper chronicled not only events of the war veterans post, but it also became a history of the neighborhood around St. Benedict Church near East (now Martin Luther King Jr.) Boulevard and Buckeye Road. Shown here are members of the newspaper's staff (from left to right) Ed Skarupa, Eugene Jonovich, George Rudy, John St. John, and John Lenard. (Courtesy of Jan Zamiska.)

With its commander, Ray Zamiska, leading the way, members of Post 381 of the Catholic War Veterans march on East (now Martin Luther King Jr.) Boulevard at Forest Avenue in 1952. Members of Post 381 marched on a number of occasions, including Memorial Day. (Courtesy of Jan Zamiska.)

The Slovak League of America represents a large portion of organized Americans of Slovak ancestry. Shown on the league's 60th anniversary in 1967 are, from left to right, (first row) Cleveland water commissioner Steve Suhajcik, Fr. Mikulas Sprinc (Slovak poet), Parma mayor Steve Zona, and Fr. Andrew Pier, OSB (director of the Slovak Institute); (second row) Andrej Pavelchak (secretary of the Slovak League of America Ohio District), Andrew Roman (president of the American Slovak Zemplin Social Club), Cleveland councilman Richard Harmody, Stefan Hudac (president of the Slovak Catholic Federation Ohio District), and Andrew Hudak Jr. (president of the Slovak League of America Ohio District). (Courtesy of the Slovak Institute and Library.)

Six

WORK, FAMILIES, NEIGHBORHOODS

This 1890 photograph of American Steel and Wire's central furnaces and docks gives a good idea of how close the plant was to mill workers' homes on the west bank of the Cuyahoga River. Slovaks living on Cleveland's south side (Tremont) often found work here. Built on the Cuyahoga River, the plant manufactured steel from the iron ore brought in by freighters. (Courtesy of the Cleveland Public Library, Photograph Collection.)

This panorama of the Newburgh Works of American Steel and Wire Company taken from East 93rd Street looking west shows not only the expanse of this mill but also how close it was to workers' homes. The mill, which at one time stretched from Harvard Avenue almost to Aetna Road west of East 93rd Street, was just a few doors away from boardinghouses on

Cambridge or Way Avenues, where some of the men were living. Note the clothes hanging to dry on the left. (Courtesy of the Cleveland Press Archives—Cleveland State University Library Special Collections.)

Young boys gather outside the gate of the Newburgh Works of American Steel and Wire Company in this scene from the 1890s—about the time that Slovaks had started to move into this area near Aetna and Woodland Hills Avenue (East 93rd Street). (Courtesy of the Cleveland Press Archives—Cleveland State University Library Special Collections.)

It was not long after Slovaks settled into a neighborhood that retail establishments and other businesses sprang up to serve their countrymen. The area on the southeast side of Cleveland near Nativity BVM parish is a clear indication of Slovak entrepreneurial spirit as shown in these advertisements in the Nativity annual report for 1912. Shown here is an advertisement for Ondrej Jurcak's store at East 93rd Street and Sandusky Avenue. (Courtesy of John T. Sabol.)

Ondrej Jurcak
Mäsiar a grocerista

— otvoril —

nový, čistý obchod.

V čís. 3737 E. 93. S. E.

Nie každý, kto barví lacno barví dobre!
Velmi dobre i velmi lacno barvia

Gaduš & Ungvarský

zkušení a dovední

Farbiari a Maliari

Na jare započnú barviť viacero domov   Zamýšlite-li barviť Váš dom, obráťte sa ku nim o rozpočet.   Krásne obarvený dom má väčšiu cennu a drevo často barvené nehnije.   Tiež vkusne varnišujú a grajnujú — zkuste ich na nejakú prácu.

This advertisement for Gaduš and Ungvarský, "painters and dyers," appeared in the Nativity BVM annual report in 1912. It states in part, "not everyone who paints cheap, paints well. They [Gadus and Ungvarsky] paint well and cheap . . . A nicely painted house is worth more, and often painted wood doesn't decay." (Courtesy of John T. Sabol.)

The Tatra Savings and Loan, a longtime institution in Cleveland's Slovak community, was founded in 1909 on East 23rd Street above a poolroom owned by the John Sotak family. Sotak, who immigrated to the United States in 1892, and several other businessmen organized the savings and loan to provide their countrymen and others with a safe place for their savings. (Courtesy of the Slovak Institute and Library.)

John Sotak, seated second from the right, is shown with his family, including (from left to right) his mother-in-law Susan Krizovensky, wife Mary, son George, daughter Helen, and son Charles. Standing, from left to right, are children Frank, Mary, Joseph, and John Jr. (Courtesy of the Slovak Institute and Library.)

After establishing a west side branch at West 20th Street and Abbey Avenue, Tatra Savings established what would become its main office at Woodhill Road and Sophia Avenue in 1924. By 1925, Tatra's assets exceeded $1 million. Tatra weathered the Great Depression and was one of 22 Greater Cleveland financial institutions to reopen. Tatra changed its name to State Savings in 1946 and in 1952 moved its main office to South Euclid Avenue. According to the *Encyclopedia of Cleveland History*, in 1986 the Federal Savings and Loan Insurance Corporation arranged the sale of State Savings to First Nationwide Bank of San Francisco after State encountered financial difficulties. (Courtesy of the Slovak Institute and Library.)

A grocery store on every corner and a bar on every other corner helped to make life good for Cleveland's Slovak community. Bidlencik's Saloon on West Seventh Street near University Road was a frequent stop for mill workers and others. Shown behind the bar in 1918 are, from left to right, Anna Sotak Bidlencik, Anna Bidlencik Galik, Paul Bidlencik Jr., Paul Bidlencik, and Mary Bidlencik Hennel. (Courtesy of Eileen Sotak.)

Mary Antonik Bidlencik (shown here in 1918), who lived on Forest Avenue with her seven children, experienced the plight of many Slovak wives whose husbands died at a young age. Like Mary, many had chickens, rabbits, and other small animals, which they raised in their yards for food. Her granddaughter, Dorothy Potosnak Sotak, vividly remembers catching a glimpse of the chicken's demise. (Courtesy of Eileen Sotak.)

Even birthday parties were a new experience for Slovaks in America. Dorothy Potosnak in a homemade party hat and Ted Billings celebrate Ted's third birthday party at his house on East (Martin Luther King Jr.) Boulevard, near Buckeye Road, around 1926. Ted's family legally changed their name from Bidlencik to Billings in the 1930s to have an American-sounding name. (Courtesy of Eileen Sotak.)

A trip to the country was always a treat for Slovak children growing up in the Buckeye Road area. Dorothy Potosnak strikes a pose at the Hlebak farm at Auburn Center around 1929. Sophie Antonik Hlebak was Dorothy's great-aunt. Dorothy's great-grandfather John Antonik also lived there, and Dorothy often saw him lead their blind horse with a carrot at the end of a stick. (Courtesy of Eileen Sotak.)

Anna Bidlencik Galik poses in a friend's World War I military hat in front of her parents' saloon on West Seventh Street near University Road in 1921. (Courtesy of Eileen Sotak.)

Brothers George, Edward, and John Tindira are shown in the 1940s near the Tindira family house on West Fifth Street near Literary Avenue in the Tremont area. The street overlooks the many factories in Cleveland's flats, including a tool manufacturer. According to one story, the tool company had to put screens on its windows so employees would not throw screwdrivers out the window to be picked up later for their personal use. (Courtesy of Raymond Tindira.)

Another popular Tremont area watering hole was the Checkerboard Grill, near West 14th Street and Starkweather Avenue, owned by George and Dorothy Sotak. Shown here around 1947 are, from left to right, George Sotak, Walter Grady, and Steve Sotak. George and Dorothy, their children, and Dorothy's parents, Paul and Mary Potosnak, lived on the second level above the grill. (Courtesy of Eileen Sotak.)

As shown on this certificate from St. Ladislas Church, Paul Potosnak and Maria Bidlencik were married on October 25, 1922. Paul Potosnak was a boarder at the home of Paul Bidlencik, Maria's uncle, in the Tremont area. He met his wife-to-be on a visit to her family, who lived in the Slovak area near Buckeye Road. Maria was born in Wilkes-Barre, Pennsylvania, and Paul was born in what is now Hodkovce, Slovakia. (Courtesy of Eileen Sotak.)

John Hopko (left) and his wife Elizabeth (second from right) owned a funeral home that still bears the family name today. John Hopko also owned houses on nearby Cambridge and Way Avenues, where newly arrived immigrants would live while they worked at nearby mills. The Hopkos are shown here with an unidentified married couple during the early years of the funeral home, founded in 1913. (Courtesy of John Hopko.)

The Hopko Funeral Home was originally located on East 93rd Street between Orleans and Anderson Avenues, with the Hopkos living on the first floor. Because most families held wakes in their own homes, the building was rarely used for business purposes. When it was, the Hopko family moved out for a couple of days while the bereaved family took over the first floor for the wake. (Courtesy of John Hopko.)

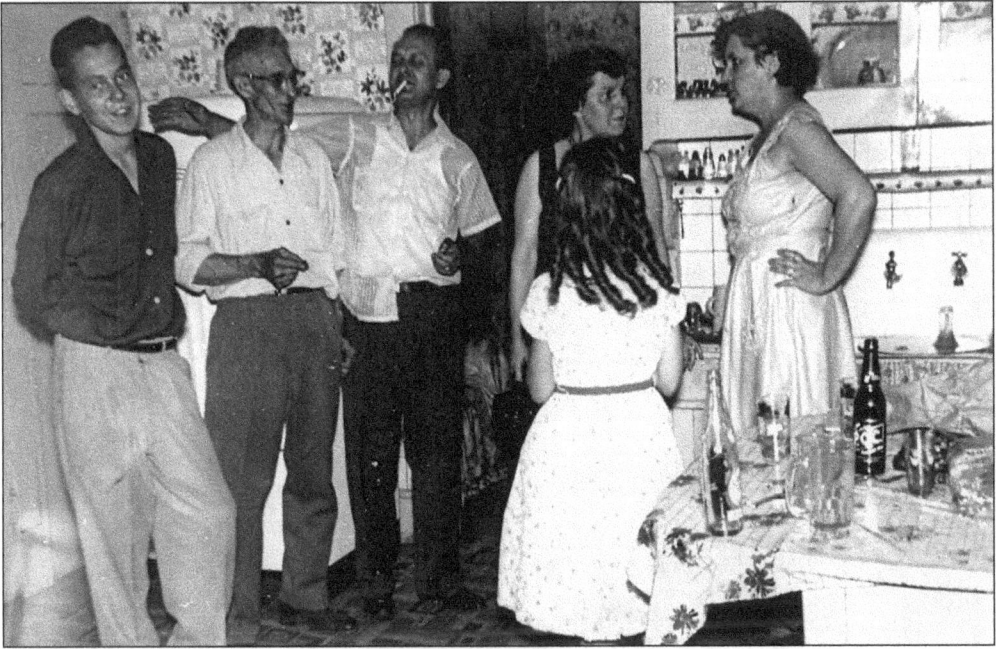

For holidays or any big occasion in the home, the kitchen became the staging area for grandma's buffet in the dining room. But it also became the gathering place for guests. At the home of Simon and Sabina Fasko on East 51st Street near Dalton Avenue, Bernie Herman, Foster Herman, John Fasko Sr., Ann Fasko Herman, and Mary Kahoun Fasko socialize before dinner. (Courtesy of Ellen Howard.)

For many years the center of one of Cleveland's Slovak/Hungarian neighborhoods was East 116th Street and Buckeye Road. In their early years in the city, relations between the two ethnic groups reflected attitudes learned in Europe. But because their businesses, churches, and other institutions were all within a several-square-mile area, they learned to coexist. (Courtesy of St. Andrew Abbey.)

The St. Benedict eighth-grade baseball team is shown in 1930 with Fr. Leo Rehak, OSB, pastor, after winning a championship trophy, possibly from the Knights of Columbus. Shown from left to right are (first row) Paul Kopco, ? Seremet, Bill Dziak, Fr. Leo Rehak, OSB, Emil Hornack, and Anthony Virost; (second row) George Klimko, Tom Smolko, Red ?, Steve Rehak, Andy Meluch, and Steve Knotek. (Courtesy of James Virost.)

Anthony Virost stands with his son Jim in about 1947 in front of the bar he and his brothers owned on Carnegie Avenue. A World War II veteran, Tony grew up in St. Benedict parish near Buckeye Road, marrying Celia Rossy. The bar continued for several years after this photograph was taken, and Jim would later remember visiting the tavern on Sundays to wash glasses from the night before. (Courtesy of James Virost.)

Andrew Ferenc (right) is shown on the job at the US Steel (American Steel and Wire) Corporation's Cuyahoga Works preparing a load of steel for shipping. Born in Kassabela, Hungary (now Košická Belá, Slovakia), he came to the United States at age nine with his mother in 1920. His father had originally immigrated in 1911, and the two never met until 1920. Both father and son worked at one time at the Newburgh Works of American Steel and Wire, a US Steel subsidiary later absorbed by the parent company in 1964. (Courtesy of Edward Ferenc.)

The National Carbon Company (later Union Carbide and now GrafTech International) was the magnet that drew Slovaks to Lakewood. Built in 1892, the plant started to attract Slovak workers from the west side of Cleveland. National Carbon had excess land west of its plant (bottom of photograph), which it sold to workers at cheap prices. Cut through with streets named Robin, Plover, Thrush, and similar names, the area quickly acquired the nickname Birdtown. This view looks east along Madison Avenue. Magee Avenue, at the eastern end of Birdtown, can be seen at the bottom. (Courtesy of the Lakewood Historical Society.)

As Lakewood's Slovak community grew, homegrown businesses also grew along Madison Avenue. These included the Orol Federal Savings and Loan Association at 12511 Madison. The predecessor of Home Federal Savings Bank, Orol (eagle in Slovak) was the first locally owned bank in Lakewood. Through a series of acquisitions, Home Federal is now part of Charter One, which is owned by the Royal Bank of Scotland. (Courtesy of the Lakewood Historical Society.)

Also known as the "Carbon District" because of the proximity of the National Carbon (Union Carbide) plant, Madison Avenue in Lakewood sprouted a number of homegrown businesses. Shown in this 1940 view between Lakewood and Ridgewood Avenues are the law offices of George Fedor, Samuel Stoyanoff's meat market, Andrew Gamary's barbershop, Cort Shoes, Mansky's Shoes, and Fisher Foods grocery store. (Courtesy of the Lakewood Historical Society.)

Many Slovaks who took jobs at National Carbon on West 117th Street originally lived farther away. But the company eventually bought land between West 117th Street and Madison Park, which it sold to its workers. Several streets bore bird's names, so the area became known as Birdtown. Some workers who had come to the United States without their families might have stayed at this boardinghouse on Plover Avenue. (Courtesy of John T. Sabol.)

This building on Quail Avenue in Lakewood was known as Cifranic's Hall and would have been the site of many weddings and other big celebrations in Birdtown. Many initial homeowners in Birdtown were Slovak Lutherans who quickly set out to establish churches for themselves. Earning only $1 to $1.50 a day, they managed to care for their families and establish residences. (Courtesy of John T. Sabol.)

90

Seven

LIFE'S JOYS

This scene shows the spacious playground for children at Nativity BVM parish, where a group of schoolgirls is playing baseball. The Nativity school student population was quickly growing as Slovak immigrants were still arriving to work in nearby steel mills and foundries. (Courtesy of the Slovak Institute and Library.)

Children enjoy the swings at the Nativity BVM playground around 1915. As newcomers in the neighborhood, the Slovaks of Nativity were sometimes met with resistance by non-Slovak neighbors. The story goes that the sounds of children playing on the swings annoyed someone so much that they came at night to cut the ropes that held the swings. (Courtesy of Nativity BVM Parish.)

Fr. Vaclav Chaloupka, Nativity BVM pastor from 1908 to 1956, purchased property on Kelleys Island around 1920. He established the acreage as a summer retreat—later a camp—for children of the parish. Shown here is one of the earliest groups to visit Kelleys Island from the early 1920s. (Courtesy of the Slovak Institute and Library.)

These boys and girls are shown at an outing at Fr. Vaclav Chaloupka's camp on Kelleys Island—probably in the early 1920s, when time spent away from the city and by Lake Erie was usually a reward for perfect attendance at school or good penmanship. (Courtesy of Joan Kovalcik.)

Time spent on Kelleys Island with Nativity BVM parish's Fr. Vaclav Chaloupka was not without its share of work. Besides fun in the sun and water, children and young adults helped with various farming chores, including harvesting some hay. Their Slovak parents, used to an agrarian lifestyle, would have approved. (Courtesy of the Slovak Institute and Library.)

Cleveland Slovaks took part in the City of Cleveland All-National Exposition from March 18 to 23, 1929. While Emma Shranko modeled a Slovak bride's head covering, Julia Hruska (dressed as a boy) and Helen Zachar impersonated a Slovak peasant couple. (Courtesy of the Cleveland Public Library, Photograph Collection.)

Here is another photograph of Julia Hruska in traditional Slovak women's clothes from January 1929. (Courtesy of the Cleveland Public Library, Photograph Collection.)

94

By the 1930s, Cleveland's Slovak community had established itself. But many of their children continued many of the old country traditions as shown in this photograph from June 1930. In costume are these Slovak dancers, from left to right, Evelyn Horvath, Martha Kolar, Antonette Horvath, Mary Ann Grega, Mary Grega, and Mary Horvath. (Courtesy of the Cleveland Public Library, Photograph Collection.)

Anne Vatrt, of 6514 Metta Avenue, a Slovak born in Austria-Hungary, is shown with her American-born daughter Mary in costume from the Slovak town of Straze nad Vahom near Bratislava. (Courtesy of the Cleveland Public Library, Photograph Collection.)

Mary Pazicky displays some Slovak embroidery, which was shown at the All-National Exposition sponsored by the Cleveland Press and the City of Cleveland from March 18 to 23, 1929. More than 31 houses representing Cleveland's various ethnic groups were on display and contained artwork valued at $1 million. (Courtesy of the Cleveland Public Library, Photograph Collection.)

Taking part in the Cleveland Press/City of Cleveland All-National Exposition is Mary Komar, showing how thread is made out of flax. The method she is using was described as that used by women in Slovak villages. (Courtesy of the Cleveland Public Library, Photograph Collection.)

Marie Brinda of Lakewood shows off the dress she is wearing to the Parade of Nations, held on July 4, 1933, at Gordon Park in Cleveland. Fourteen nationality groups, including Slovaks, took part in the festivities. (Courtesy of the Cleveland Public Library, Photograph Collection.)

The 1930s and the Depression saw a bigger role for Slovak parishes as community anchors, and St. Wendelin Parish was no different. In April 1932, Klub Sv. Tomas (St. Thomas) of St. Wendelin's presented the play *Slovensky Mucedelnese Ktore Oddochow Dramaticki*. (Courtesy of St. Wendelin Church.)

A capacity group of about 100 girls spent a week at the Villa, the Nativity school summer camp on Kelleys Island in 1939. Fees for each were $7 for children under 14 and $8 for children over 14, plus $1.50 boat fare. Besides water and nature activities, the camp also had a roller-skating rink and tennis courts. The boys shown in this photograph were probably sons of mothers who had volunteered to work at the camp. (Courtesy of Archives, Diocese of Cleveland.)

Because his mother was helping out at the Nativity school summer camp on Kelleys Island in 1938, young Daniel Sabol was able to tag along, even though he may have been too young to join the regular campers. (Courtesy of John T. Sabol.)

As the Villa, Fr. Vaclav Chaloupka's camp on Kelleys Island, grew during the 1930s, he enlisted men and women of the parish to assist in running it. Many stayed the summer and had the chance to watch their children enjoy the fresh air away from the polluted city. Doing the laundry in 1938 are Nativity parishioners Florence Sabol and Agnes Cech. (Courtesy of John T. Sabol.)

When Fr. Vaclav Chaloupka purchased his Kelleys Island property, it was already bordered by a stone wall. As years progressed, he expanded the wall and kept it in repair by taking flat rocks out of the soil near the camp and adding them to the wall. The labor, of course, was done by campers, who helped pull the rocks out, and adult parishioners (shown here), who found the right spots for the stones. (Courtesy of John T. Sabol.)

One of the largest and oldest Slovak social clubs in Greater Cleveland is the American Slovak Zemplin Social Club, consisting mainly of Cleveland Slovaks from historic Zemplin County in the eastern portion of what is now Slovakia. This early photograph of the club, which was founded in 1941, shows members outside Holy Ghost Byzantine Church in Tremont in costumes depicting members of a Slovak wedding. (Courtesy of the American Slovak Zemplin Social Club.)

At one time, Cleveland had a number of clubs representing other Slovak counties where the city's Slovak Americans were born. The American Slovak Zemplin Social Club is the only surviving club. This photograph from the late 1950s or early 1960s depicts a typical Slovak wedding. (Courtesy of the American Slovak Zemplin Social Club.)

In Cleveland's Slovak neighborhoods, the church—usually Roman Catholic—became the anchor for the community. Young and old parishioners at Nativity BVM parish had the advantage of two bowling alleys (shown here in the late 1940s), a large gymnasium, two large social halls, and two meeting rooms—all in the parish school. (Courtesy of John T. Sabol.)

No matter the project or event, Nativity BVM parishioners could be counted on to make it happen. This group of women from the 1950s gets ready for a parish dinner—possibly an anniversary celebration. Each year, mothers of the parish also prepared a banquet for the children of the school. (Courtesy of Archives, Diocese of Cleveland.)

Dressed in native costumes and admiring needlework held by Alice Toth (seated center) are (clockwise, from left to right) Emma Krinos, Ellen Zazik, Ann Sulovsky, and Mary Strbo. (Courtesy of the Cleveland Public Library, Photograph Collection.)

These members of the Slovak Dancing Club were part of the entertainment on June 23, 1968, at the 32nd annual American Slovak Day, sponsored by the American-Slovak Activities Committee of Northern Ohio. Shown from left to right are dancers Joseph Novak, Helene Baco, and sisters Georgine, Ann, and Therese Palisin. (Photograph by Paul Toppelstein, courtesy of the Cleveland Press Archives—Cleveland State University Library Special Collections.)

The first cultural day celebration at Our Lady of Mercy parish coincided with the U.S. bicentennial celebration in 1976. According to the parish's 75th anniversary history, it was the only church in the United States whose events were recorded in the written *United States Bicentennial History*. Shown here is a demonstration of Slovak rug making. (Courtesy of Jim Noga.)

No Slovak family with its own sausage-stuffer would dream of buying the store-bought stuff, and the Fasko household on Alameda Avenue in Lakewood in 1980 was no different. Brothers Jacob and Joseph Fasko are laboring over a batch of kolbasi. (Courtesy of Ellen Howard.)

Eight

WHERE THERE
IS A SLOVAK,
THERE IS A SONG

The Krivan Dramatic Club was formed out of the Krivan Choir, the oldest Slovak choir in the United States, founded in 1906 by Miloslav Francisci, the son of a famous Slovak writer, who immigrated to Cleveland in 1886. Besides directing Krivan, he composed a number of dramas and operettas in Slovak. This is a tableau from the group's 1918 production, *Obsitosova Dcera*. (Courtesy of the Slovak Institute and Library.)

Fr. Vaclav Chaloupka, pastor of Nativity BVM parish (fourth from the right), is shown with members of the National Slovak Band and others at an outing—probably from the early 1920s. A number of U.S. communities, including Webster, Massachusetts, and Windber, Pennsylvania, had also established "national" bands, and Cleveland was no different. (Courtesy of the Slovak Institute and Library.)

This group of Slovak men took part in the All-Nations pageant held on September 3, 1928, at Edgewater Park in Cleveland. Shown from left to right in what was described as a dance of the forests are (first row) Samuel Galik, George Simon, and John Keleciny; (second row) Julius Diamska, Frank Butchko, Vladimir Vitous, and Andrew Kopcok. (Courtesy of the Cleveland Press Archives—Cleveland State University Library Special Collections.)

These Slovak dancers dressed in native costumes prepare for one of the many events that celebrated Cleveland's diverse ethnic heritage. The venerable Slovak photographer Joseph Bachna took this photograph. (Courtesy of the Cleveland Press Archives—Cleveland State University Library Special Collections.)

Old country traditions handed down from parents to children were evident as the older generation and their offspring participated in Czecho-Slovak Day at Ceska Sin Sokol Hall on Clark Avenue on August 8, 1927. Getting ready to perform a Slovak folk dance are (from left to right) Anna Boszak and Angela Bachna. (Courtesy of the Cleveland Press Archives—Cleveland State University Library Special Collections.)

The Slovak Dramatic Club, still an important part of the Cleveland Slovak community, was established in 1949. Besides presenting live cultural programs, the club raised thousands of dollars to aid Slovak refugees scattered throughout Europe during the 1950s. Shown here are members of the Slovak Dramatic Club singing during a One World Day program at the Slovak Cultural Garden in the 1950s. (Courtesy of the Cleveland Public Library, Photograph Collection.)

Mrs. M. Sovish, Paul Valach, Julia Lamar, and John Trhan strike a pose as part of a Slovak dance group at a Cleveland nationalities festival in November 1927. (Courtesy of the Cleveland Public Library, Photograph Collection.)

An old Slovak tradition is the traveling carolers or Jaslickari—men who would go door to door during the time after Christmas to sing Christmas carols for friends and neighbors, cause a little mischief, and perhaps get some Christmas sweets or—better yet—a glass of Christmas cheer. In the early 1950s, members of the Slovak Dramatic Club carried on this tradition. Shown from left to right are John Sopko, Michael Valco, Vincent Jacko, Joseph Hudak, and Andrew Hudak. (Courtesy of the Slovak Institute and Library.)

An annual event at Nativity BVM parish, celebrated up to the closing of the parish in 1992, was the children's Christmas pageant, which took place before Midnight Mass on Christmas. Children memorized and sang Slovak Christmas carols and reenacted the Christmas story. The pageant concluded with angels, shepherds, and peasant girls gathered around the manger, shown here in the 1930s. (Courtesy of John T. Sabol.)

Angels announce the birth of Jesus by singing in Slovak during the Nativity BVM Christmas pageant—shown here in 1946. (Courtesy of Archives, Diocese of Cleveland.)

The Nativity BVM Christmas pageant involved the entire space of Nativity church, with young boys dressed as shepherds and girls dressed as peasants processing and singing Slovak Christmas carols. This pageant took place in 1946. (Courtesy of Archives, Diocese of Cleveland.)

Seventh- and eighth-grade boys from Nativity BVM school were usually selected to take the parts of shepherds in the annual Christmas Eve Christmas pageant. Armed with lanterns and shepherds crooks, these boys help to reenact the Christmas story in this scene from 1946. (Courtesy of Archives, Diocese of Cleveland.)

The Ferko Orchestra of Cleveland performed on the Slovak Radio Hour, which was broadcast from WJAY in Akron. The orchestra actually performed in a remote broadcast from the stage of the Fox Tele-News Theater on Euclid Avenue in Cleveland. Shown from left to right are Charlie Dudash (trombone), Frank Mihaly (violin), John Bobko (piano), Joe Ibosh (banjo), Joe Toth (trumpet), and Andrew Ferko (clarinet). Two other groups, Sedlak's Orchestra and the Joseph Pales Orchestra, also performed. (Courtesy of Andrew Ferko.)

A venerable Slovak saying states that "where there is a Slovak, there is a song." And the Fasko household on East 51st Street near Dalton Avenue was no different. This scene from the 1950s shows, from left to right, Simon Fasko playing the bass fiddle, Foster Herman, Helen Fasko Marzec, and John Fasko Sr. playing the fiddle. (Courtesy of Ellen Howard.)

Taking part in the 39th Slovak Day at Puritas Spring Park, held on June 26, 1955, are Mary Rodak and Edward Ferenc, playing the *fujara*. The event was sponsored by the Slovak Catholic Federation and the Slovak League of America. (Courtesy of the Cleveland Press Archives—Cleveland State University Library Special Collections.)

Combining baking and the arts is not out of the ordinary for some Slovak groups, including the Gen. Milan Stefanik Singing and Dramatic Club. Shown here are club members Ann Williams and Mrs. Vladimir Krivos with an array of baked goods made from Slovak recipes. (Courtesy of the Cleveland Public Library, Photograph Collection.)

Because of Cleveland's high concentration of Slovaks and Czechs, the city has always been a magnet for touring groups, particularly from Czechoslovakia and now the Slovak and Czech republics. In December 1964, the Czechoslovak State Folk Dance Group appeared at the Cleveland Arena to present characteristic dances from Bohemia, Moravia, and Slovakia. The group's appearance in Cleveland at that time was viewed as a sign that the Iron Curtain countries wanted to establish more contacts in the United States. (Courtesy of the Cleveland Press Archives—Cleveland State University Library Special Collections.)

Another Slovak dance group formed during the 1970s was a group called Travnica, founded by the late Paul Janko, whose roots in Slovakia were in Nižná Polianka and Belá nad Cirochou. Shown in March 1979 are Denise Ivan and Joseph Verba of Parma and Heidi and Joseph Fornadel of Orange Village. (Photograph by Herman Seid, courtesy of the Cleveland Press Archives— Cleveland State University Library Special Collections.)

Our Lady of Mercy Church in Tremont continued the parish's Slovak traditions, even into the 1980s, as demonstrated by the dancers at the parish's cultural day in 1980. (Courtesy of Jim Noga.)

Shown from left to right are folk dancers at Our Lady of Mercy Church in 1947: (first row) Andrew Sparhac, Frank Medvec, James Shockles, Steve Gerda, John Homala, Donald Parrish, Ray Gordon, Ronald Yersky, and Jimmy Timko; (second row) Rita Lou Sotak, Amelia Hudac, Betty Ann Koncar, Rita Mae Voytovich, Ronald Senyak, Phyllis Minarchek, Beverly Zelenka, Carol Chopka, Joan Fabian, and Rose Mary Noga. (Courtesy of Jim Noga.)

Dressed in native Slovak costumes, young people at Our Lady of Mercy Church recall their heritage in this 1976 celebration, which would grow into a yearly cultural days event at the parish. (Courtesy of Jim Noga.)

A popular bandleader among Cleveland Slovaks is Johnny Pastirik, who is seen often at Slovak and other events featuring polka music. The Johnny Pastirik combo is shown at Our Lady of Mercy parish's 1980 cultural days. (Courtesy of Jim Noga.)

Nine

WINNERS ALL

Paul Newman? Slovak? It's true. The mother of the late Paul Newman, who was born in Cleveland in 1925, was Theresa Feckova, who was born in what is now Pticie, in eastern Slovakia. She arrived in the United States after the death of her mother and lived in Chicago before moving to Cleveland. Members of her family still reside in Pticie. (Courtesy of the Cleveland Press Archives—Cleveland State University Library Special Collections.)

Joseph Dovalovsky, seated at the right, was an early leader for the rights of Slovaks in Cleveland, assisting in organizing both the Cleveland Slovak Union and the All-Slavic League in 1902 and the Slovak National Committee in 1906. He was also instrumental in the founding of the Tatra Savings and Loan, predecessor of State Savings and Loan. (Courtesy of Cyrus and Helen Duval.)

Joseph Dovalovsky had a big hand in many construction and home-building projects in Cleveland. He is shown here as a young man (third from right), supervising a crew building a storm sewer in Cleveland. (Courtesy of Cyrus and Helen Duval.)

Johnny Risko was born in the Slovak village of Bohunice in Austria-Hungary (now western Slovakia) in 1902 and was raised in Cleveland. A heavyweight boxer, he fought from 1924 to 1940 with a record of 80 wins, 53 losses, and 7 draws. He was known as the "Rubber Man" for his ability to bounce back. He is shown here in a 1931 photograph, training for a fight with Mickey Walker, which he lost in Miami. A year later he defeated Walker at Cleveland Stadium. Risko died in 1953. (Courtesy of the Cleveland Public Library, Photograph Collection.)

Although born in Luxor, Pennsylvania, Steve Sundra moved with his parents to Cleveland, living on the southeast side. His parents came to the United States from Lenartov, Austria-Hungary. After starring in sandlot baseball and moving up through the minor leagues, Sundra was signed by the Cleveland Indians in 1932 and in 1936 by the New York Yankees. He played for the world champion Yankees team of 1938 and ran off 11 straight victories in 1939. He later played for the Washington Senators and St. Louis Browns, posting a career record of 56 wins and 41 losses. He died in 1952. (Courtesy of the Cleveland Public Library, Photograph Collection.)

Big band–era fans will remember bandleader Sammy Kaye, a Cleveland area native of Slovak descent. Sammy Kaye was born in the Birdtown area of Lakewood and later attended Rocky River High School. Kaye's original surname was Zarnocay, his father and mother immigrating to Cleveland from Austria-Hungary, now Slovakia. Kaye is shown on the right during a 1958 visit to relatives in Rocky River. Shown from left to right are his nephew Joe Beckrest of Rocky River; his sisters, Mrs. Joseph Beckrest and Marie Lester, both of Rocky River; and his niece Mrs. Wallace Clevenger of Cleveland. (Courtesy of the Cleveland Press Archives—Cleveland State University Library Special Collections.)

The Slovak Institute, headquartered at St. Andrew Svorad Abbey in Cleveland, was founded by Abbot Theodore Kojis, OSB, on October 6, 1952, shortly after he returned from a visit to Czechoslovakia. He wanted to provide a facility to assist the oppressed Slovak nation, then under Communist rule, in its fight for freedom and independence. Shown is the founding meeting of the Slovak Institute, attended by, from left to right, Fr. Andrew Pier, OSB, first director of the institute; Slovak poet and translator Karel Strmen; Dr. Francis Hrusovsky, Slovak author; Abbot Theodore; artist Joseph Cincik; and Fr. Mikulas Sprinc, author and poet. (Courtesy of the Slovak Institute and Library.)

Under the direction of its first director, Fr. Andrew Pier, OSB, the Slovak Institute became a noted repository for books and other items detailing Slovak history and literature. Its current director, Andrew Hudak, has worked to restore the Slovak Institute's world-class presence. (Courtesy of the Slovak Institute and Library.)

Avid Cleveland Indians fans are sure to have seen Cy Buynak at least once during games at Cleveland Stadium or at Jacobs (later Progressive) Field. Buynak, whose father was born in Dravce, Austria-Hungary, now Slovakia, served as clubhouse manager for the Indians from 1965 to 2006. Before that he served as assistant clubhouse manager from 1961 to 1964. Growing up on Cleveland's southeast side, Buynak attended grade school at Nativity BVM Slovak Catholic parish and graduated from Benedictine High School. Besides his clubhouse duties (shown here in 1970), he also appeared in the 1991 television movie *Babe Ruth*, and he also appears as an answer in the popular game Trivial Pursuit. (Courtesy of the Cleveland Press Archives—Cleveland State University Library Special Collections.)

Cleveland radio listeners who grew up in the late 1970s and 1980s have great memories of Ed "Flash" Ferenc, part of the WMMS Morning Zoo duo of Jeff and Flash. A first-generation Slovak American whose father was born in Košická Belá, Ed "Flash" Ferenc was born and raised on the southeast side before his family moved to Seven Hills in the mid-1960s. He honed his announcing style at Normandy High School and later at Cleveland State University, eventually landing a position at WHK Radio while still in college. Flash is still active in a number of radio ventures and as public information officer for the Cleveland Municipal Court. He and his wife, Deb, operate FlashPoint, a public relations and advertising firm. (Courtesy of Edward Ferenc.)

Visit us at
arcadiapublishing.com

....

www.ingramcontent.com/pod-product-compliance
Lightning Source LLC
Chambersburg PA
CBHW080613110426
42813CB00006B/1497